Real-Life Superpowers

RESPONSIBILITY IS A SUPERPOWER

by Mari Schuh

PEBBLE
a capstone imprint

Published by Pebble, an imprint of Capstone
1710 Roe Crest Drive, North Mankato, Minnesota 56003
capstonepub.com

Copyright © 2024 by Capstone. All rights reserved. No part of this publication may be reproduced in whole or in part, or stored in a retrieval system, or transmitted in any form or by any means, electronic, mechanical, photocopying, recording, or otherwise, without written permission of the publisher.

Library of Congress Cataloging-in-Publication Data is available on the Library of Congress website.
ISBN: 9780756576844 (hardcover)
ISBN: 9780756576790 (paperback)
ISBN: 9780756576806 (ebook PDF)

Summary: You take care of your belongings. When you make a mistake, you admit it and tell the truth. Taking responsibility can be hard, but this real-life superpower is worth it. Learn more about it and how you can be a superhero in your daily life.

Image Credits
Getty Images: iStock/PeopleImages, Cover, 4, JGI/Jamie Grill, 13, Nazar Abbas Photography, 17, skynesher, 5, 8; Shutterstock: Branislav Nenin, 7, Daisy Daisy, 11, Gatot Adri, 15, Kapitosh (background), matimix, 18, michaeljung, 19, Natallia Boroda, 20, nazarovsergey, 9, SeventyFour, 16

Editorial Credits
Editor: Alison Deering; Designer: Bobbie Nuytten; Media Researcher: Rebekah Hubstenberger; Production Specialist: Whitney Schaefer

All internet sites appearing in back matter were available and accurate when this book was sent to press.

Printed and bound in China. PO 5593

Table of Contents

Responsibility Matters 4

Being Responsible at Home 10

Being Responsible at School 14

Doing Your Best 18

    Grow Your Own Plants 20

    Glossary 22

    Read More 23

    Internet Sites 23

    Index 24

    About the Author 24

Words in **bold** are in the glossary.

Responsibility Matters

Were you **responsible** today? What did you do? Did you work hard at school? Maybe you were on time for dance class. Maybe you helped set the table before dinner.

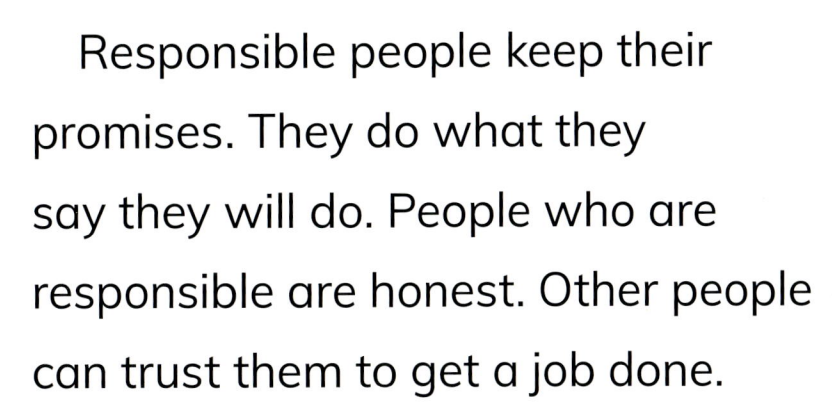

Responsible people keep their promises. They do what they say they will do. People who are responsible are honest. Other people can trust them to get a job done.

Responsibility is a **superpower**. Why? When you are responsible, you treat others fairly. People can depend on you. They know you will not let them down. This gives you **confidence**. You work hard and always do your best.

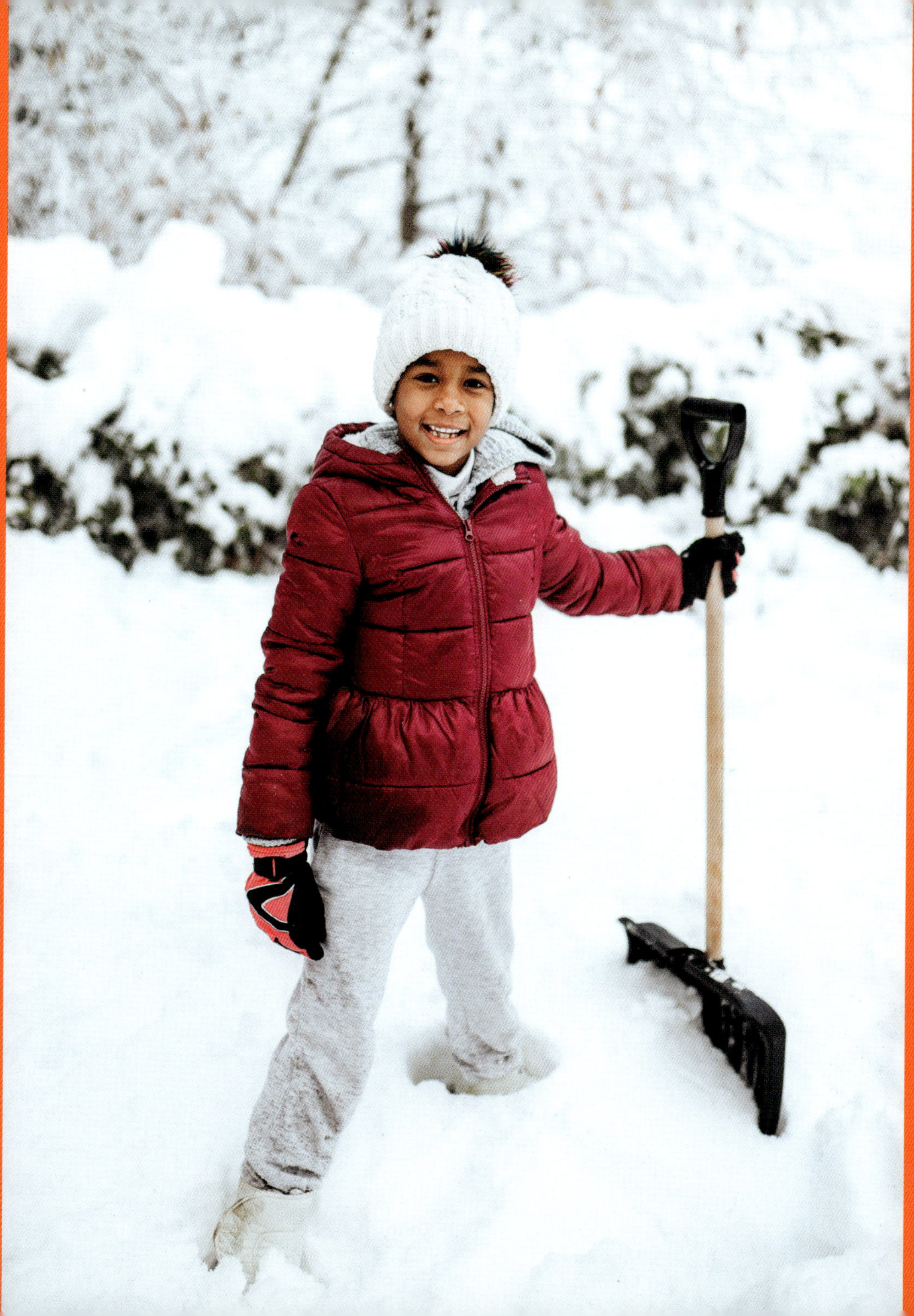

Sometimes people are not responsible. Maybe they are tired. Maybe they want to play and have fun. Or they might be too busy. They forget what they need to do.

When this happens, people are not being dependable. They might make **excuses** or **blame** other people.

Being Responsible at Home

You can be responsible at home. Clean your room without being asked. Make your bed. Put away your toys. Then your room will look great!

Being responsible takes **discipline**. It means going to bed on time. It also means doing your **chores.**

Pete does chores before he plays. He does not complain. He loads the dishwasher and sweeps the floor. Being responsible makes him feel good. Lakin folds the laundry and feeds her pet rabbit. She is proud of doing her best!

Tavon earns an **allowance** by doing extra chores. He is responsible with the money. Every week, he makes sure to save some. Tavon thinks carefully before he spends his money. He takes time to think about what he really wants to buy. He makes good choices.

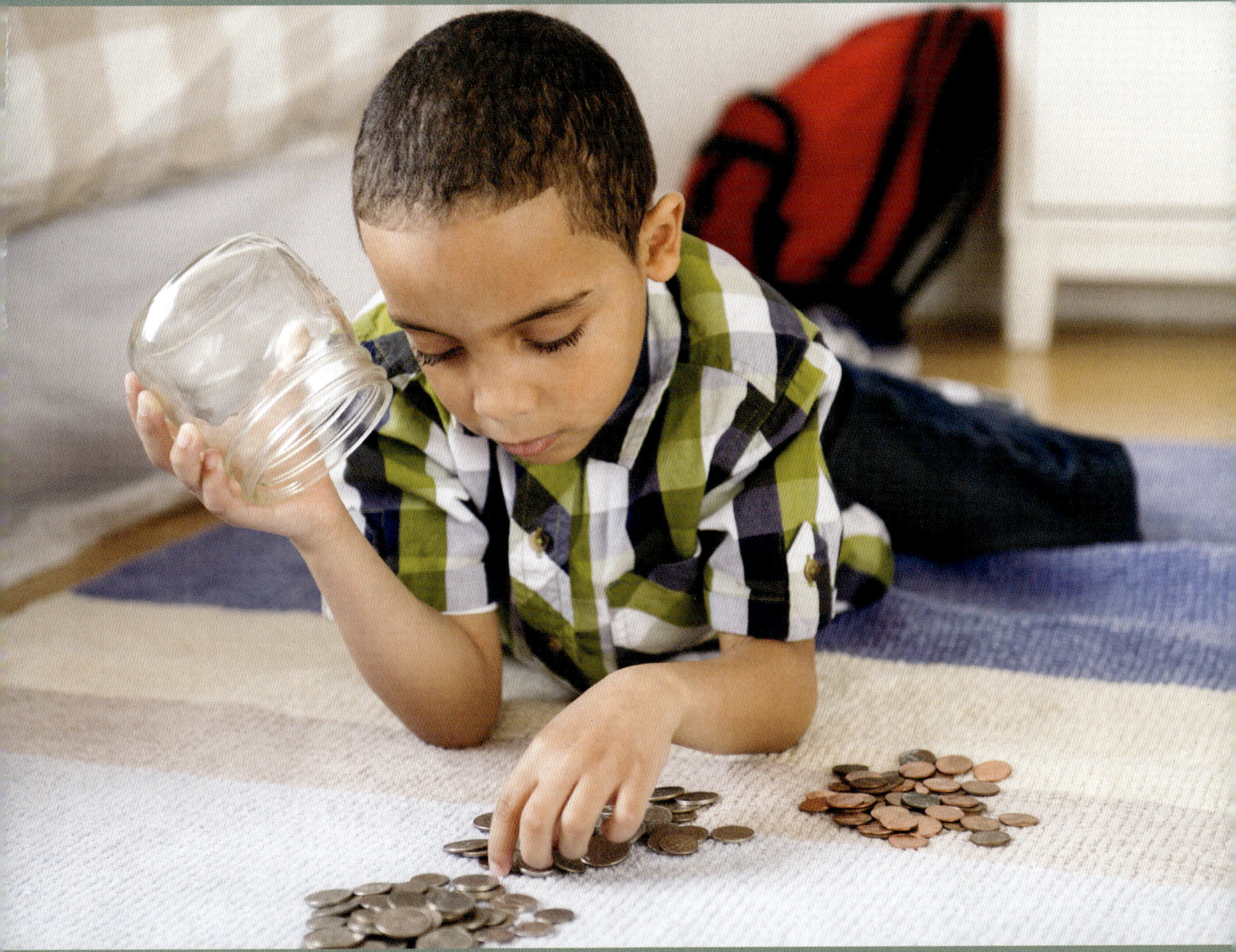

Being Responsible at School

Dele is responsible at school. She has a big project due soon. Dele does not wait until the last day to do all the work. She works on it every day. She uses a planner. She writes down what she needs to do. Dele gets her project done on time. She feels proud and happy!

Judah borrows a book from another student. He takes good care of it. He remembers to give it back when he is done. Judah is a responsible classmate.

Everyone makes mistakes. They are a part of life. Being responsible means admitting mistakes. Tess dropped a jar of paint on the floor at art class. It was a mess! Tess admits what happened. She does not blame a classmate. The class works together to clean up the paint.

Jon remembers to clean his table after lunch. He also makes sure he is on time for the soccer game. Jon **respects** his coach and teammates. He does not want to make them wait.

Doing Your Best

Being responsible takes practice. Always do your best. Don't give up. Keep your promises.

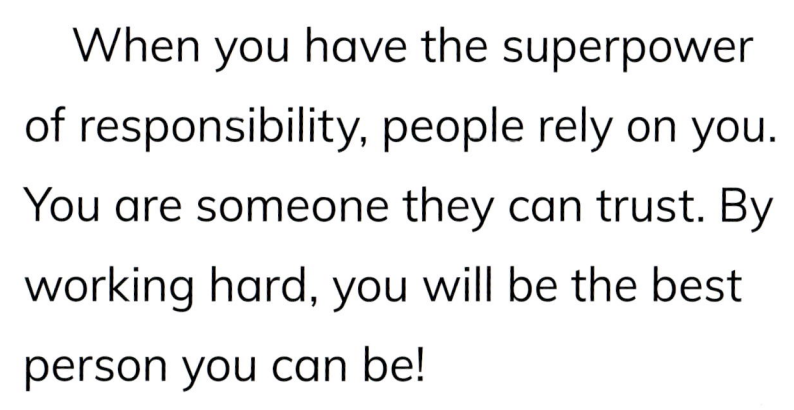

When you have the superpower of responsibility, people rely on you. You are someone they can trust. By working hard, you will be the best person you can be!

Grow Your Own Plants

Growing your own plants can be fun! It's also a great way to practice responsibility. Try this activity as a way to show your superpower.

What You Need:

- small container—a flower pot, milk carton, or egg carton
- small saucer or plastic tray
- potting mix
- seeds—try radishes, lettuce, beans, or peas
- water
- sunny windowsill

What You Do:

1. Ask an adult to punch a few small holes in the bottom of a small container. This will drain extra water. Then put the pot on a saucer or tray.

2. Fill the pot a little more than halfway with potting mix.

3. Carefully add a few seeds on top of the potting mix. Then sprinkle a little more potting mix on top. The mix should be loose, not tightly packed.

4. Lightly water the seeds.

5. Place your container on a sunny windowsill. Windows that face south or west get more light.

6. Check your pot every day. Make sure it is getting enough sunlight. Feel the potting mix. If it is dry, water the seeds.

7. Remember to take good care of your seeds every day. This is a good way to practice being responsible. Soon, the seeds will sprout! Being responsible will have paid off.

Glossary

allowance (uh-LOU-uhns)—an amount of money given on a regular basis or for a particular purpose

blame (BLAYM)—to say that what happened was someone else's fault

chore (CHOR)—a job that has to be done regularly

confidence (KON-fi-duhns)—to trust in a person or thing

discipline (DIS-uh-plin)—self-control and the ability to follow the rules

excuse (ik SKYOOS)—something offered as a reason for doing something

respect (ri-SPEKT)—to believe in the quality and worth of others and yourself

responsible (ri-SPON-suh-buhl)—doing what you say you will do

superpower (SOO-pur-pow-ur)—an important skill that can affect yourself and others in a big way

Read More

Andrews, Elizabeth. *Understanding Responsibility.* Minneapolis: Cody Koala, an imprint of Pop!, 2023.

Peters, Katie. *I Am Responsible.* Minneapolis: Lerner Publications, 2022.

Rose, Emily. *Taking Responsibility and Being a Leader.* Ann Arbor, MI: Cherry Lake Publishing, 2022.

Internet Sites

ABCYA: Learn to Count Money
abcya.com/games/counting_money

PBS Learning Media: Little Helper: Daniel Tiger's Neighborhood
https://kcts9.pbslearningmedia.org/resource/01204ad9-bbaf-4275-a35e-691d441e2eea/little-helper-daniel-tigers-neighborhood/

Talking With Trees: What Is Responsibility?
https://talkingtreebooks.com/teaching-resources-catalog/definitions/what-is-responsibility.html

Index

allowance, 12

blame, 9

chores, 4, 10, 11, 12

confidence, 6

discipline, 10

excuses, 9

fairness, 6

honesty, 5, 16

making mistakes, 16

promises, 5, 18

schoolwork, 14

trust, 5, 19

About the Author

Mari Schuh's love of reading began with cereal boxes at the kitchen table. Today she is the author of hundreds of nonfiction books for beginning readers. Mari lives in the Midwest with her husband and their sassy house rabbit. Learn more about her at marischuh.com.